BEST OF
DUKE ELLINGTON

🔊 16 SONGS WITH ONLINE AUDIO BACKING TRACKS

PLAYBACK+
Speed • Pitch • Balance • Loop

To access audio visit:
www.halleonard.com/mylibrary

Enter Code
6263-5966-9216-3372

Cover photo © Getty Images / Gjon Mili / Contributor

ISBN 978-1-5400-4622-2

HAL•LEONARD®

Visit Hal Leonard Online at
www.halleonard.com

Contact us:
Hal Leonard
7777 West Bluemound Road
Milwaukee, WI 53213
Email: info@halleonard.com

In Europe, contact:
Hal Leonard Europe Limited
42 Wigmore Street
Marylebone, London, W1U 2RN
Email: info@halleonardeurope.com

In Australia, contact:
Hal Leonard Australia Pty. Ltd.
4 Lentara Court
Cheltenham, Victoria, 3192 Australia
Email: info@halleonard.com.au

CARAVAN

Words and Music by DUKE ELLINGTON,
IRVING MILLS and JUAN TIZOL

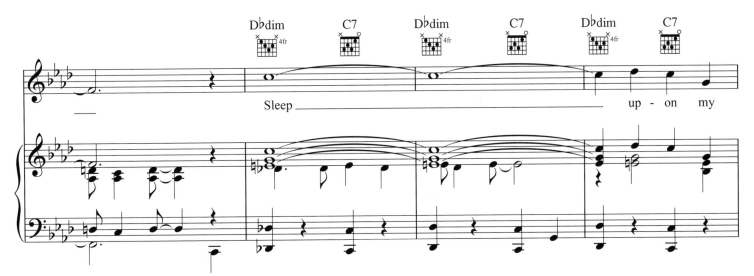

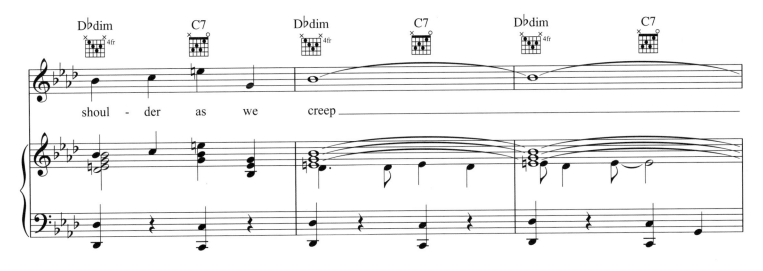

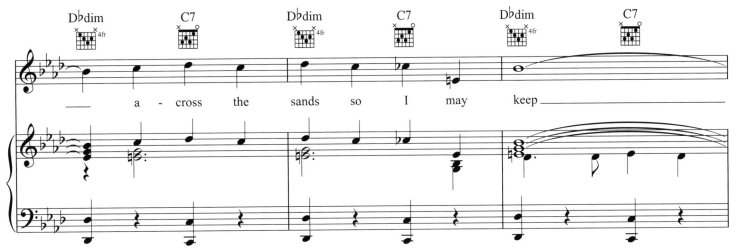

this mem-'ry of our car-a-

van.

This ____ is so ex-cit - ing

you ____ are so in-vit -

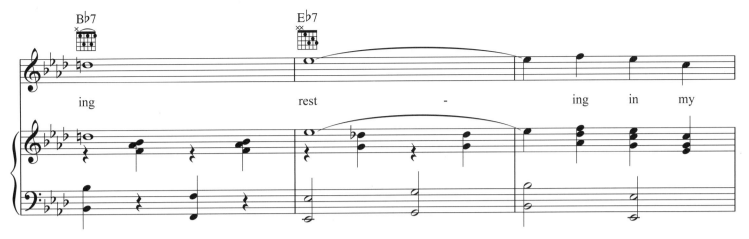

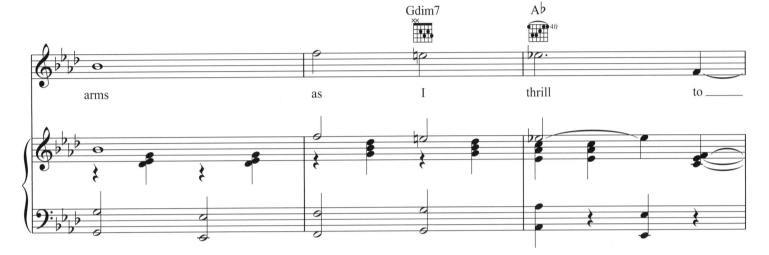

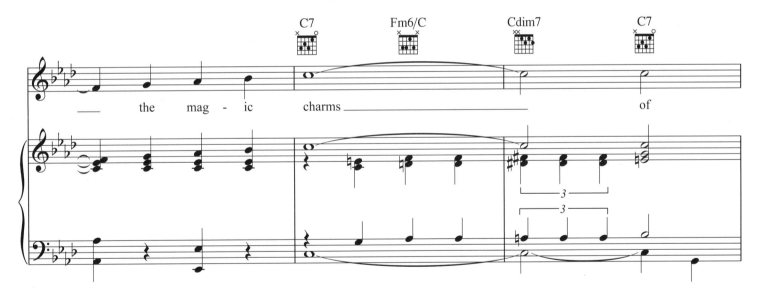

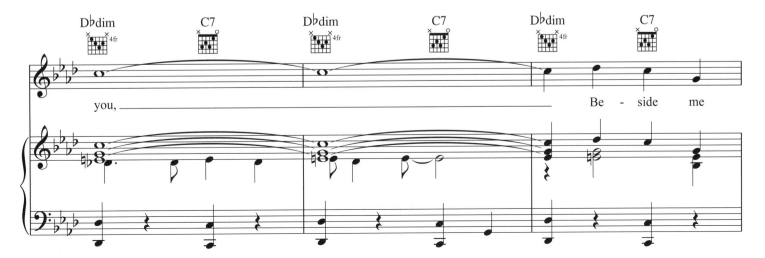

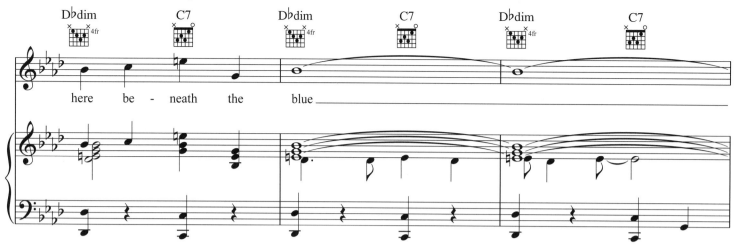

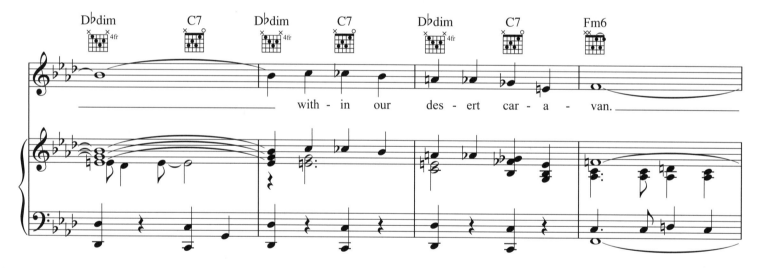

COME SUNDAY
from BLACK, BROWN & BEIGE

By DUKE ELLINGTON

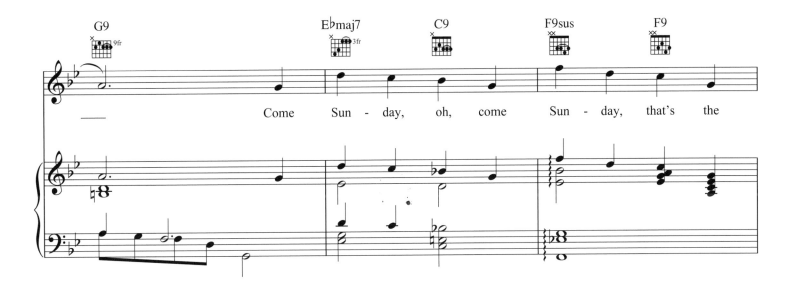

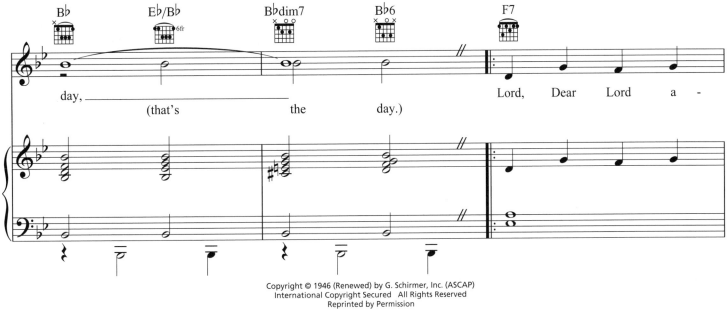

just clouds pass - ing by.
have a bright - er by and by.
through e - ter - ni - ty.
Lord, Dear Lord a -

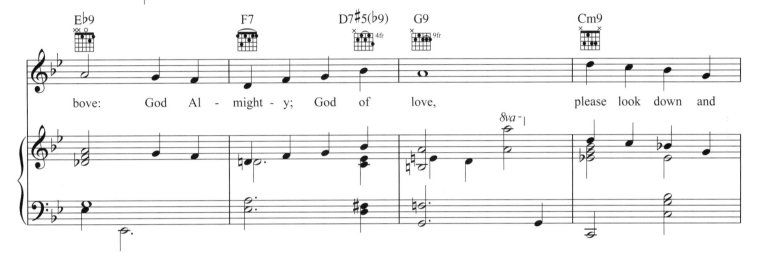

bove: God Al - might - y; God of love, please look down and

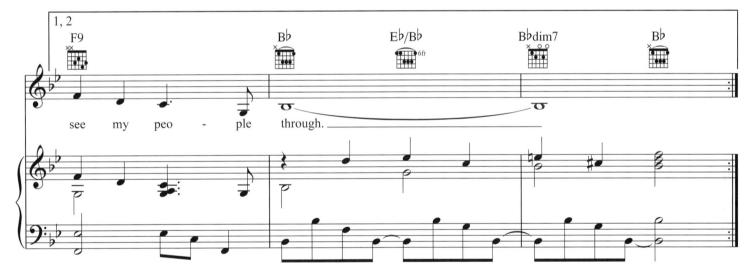

see my peo - ple through. _____

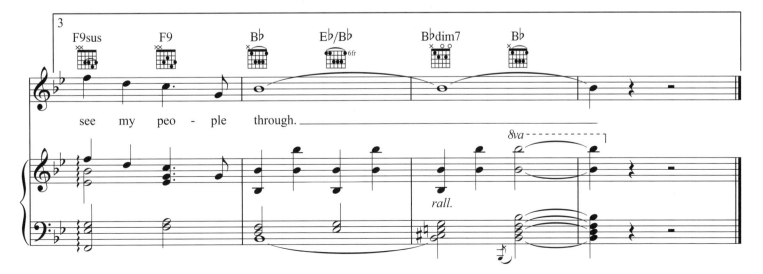

see my peo - ple through. _____

DO NOTHIN' TILL YOU HEAR FROM ME

Words and Music by DUKE ELLINGTON
and BOB RUSSELL

DON'T GET AROUND MUCH ANYMORE

Words and Music by DUKE ELLINGTON
and BOB RUSSELL

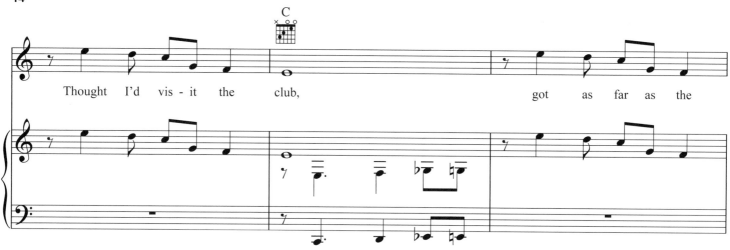

Thought I'd vis-it the club, got as far as the

door, they'd have ask'd me a-bout you, ___

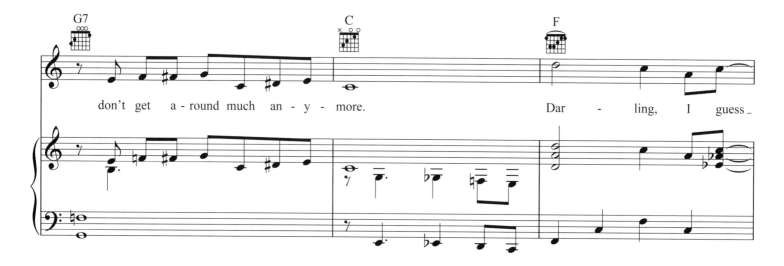

don't get a-round much an-y-more. Dar - ling, I guess ___

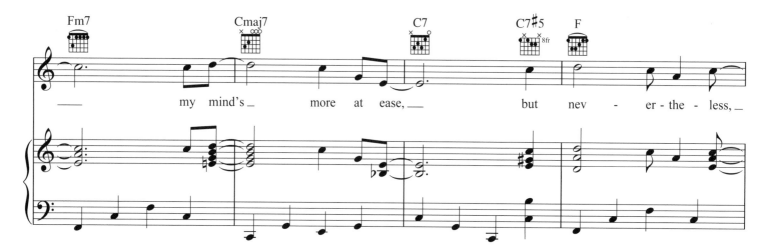

my mind's ___ more at ease, ___ but nev - er-the - less, ___

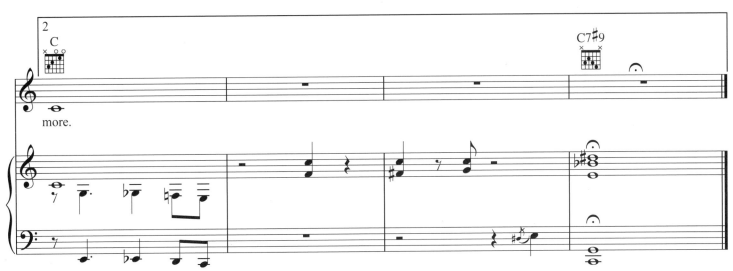

I GOT IT BAD AND THAT AIN'T GOOD

Words by PAUL FRANCIS WEBSTER
Music by DUKE ELLINGTON

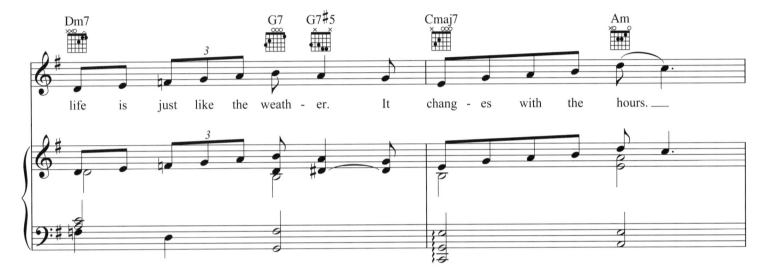

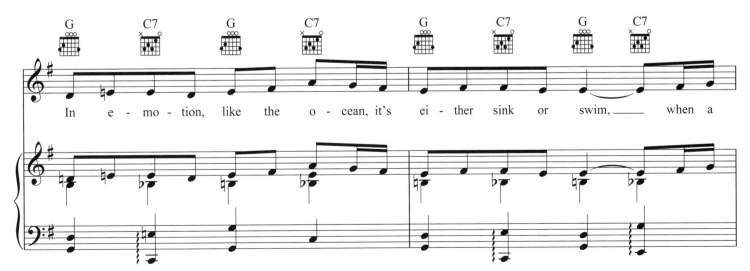

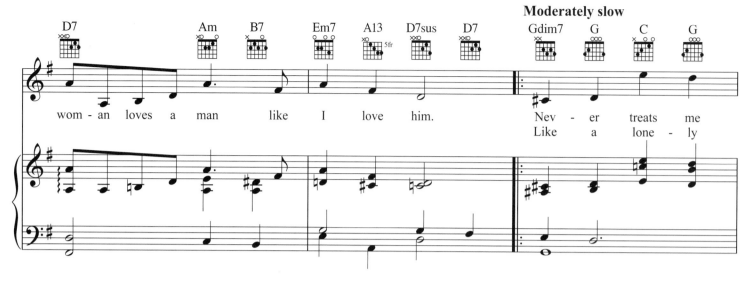

Moderately slow

wom - an loves a man like I love him. Nev - er treats me
Like a lone - ly

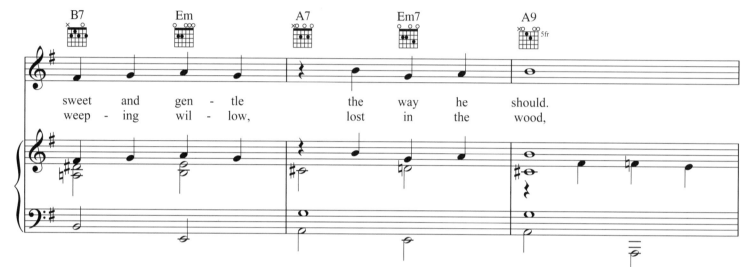

sweet and gen - tle the way he should.
weep - ing wil - low, lost in the wood,

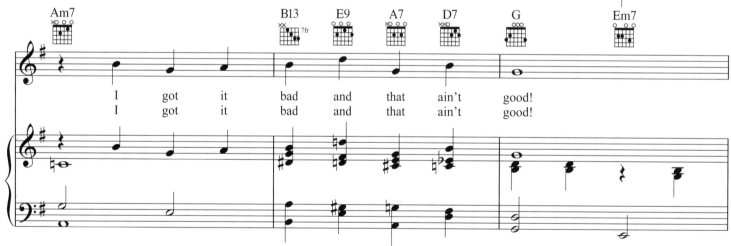

I got it bad and that ain't good!
I got it bad and that ain't good!

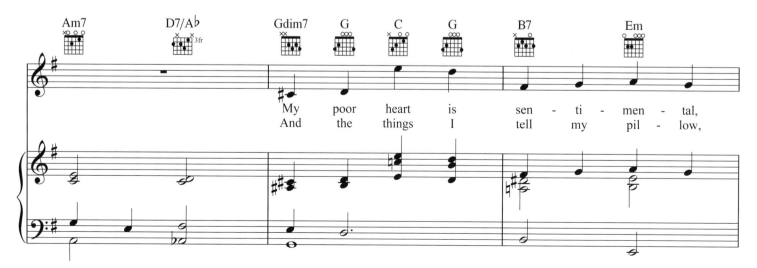

My poor heart is sen - ti - men - tal,
And the things I tell my pil - low,

I'M BEGINNING TO SEE THE LIGHT

Words and Music by DON GEORGE,
JOHNNY HODGES, DUKE ELLINGTON
and HARRY JAMES

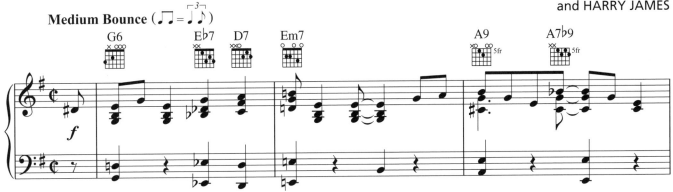

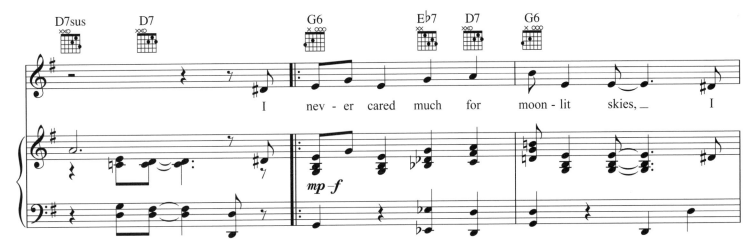

I nev-er cared much for moon-lit skies, __ I

nev-er wink back at fire-flies, __ but now that the stars are

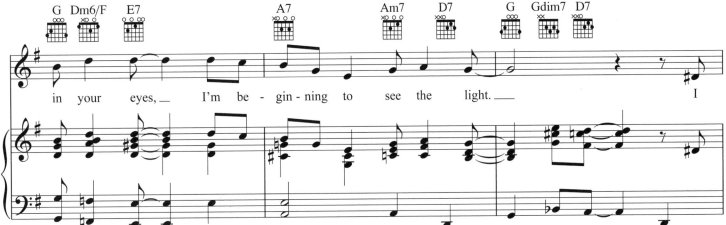

in your eyes, __ I'm be-gin-ning to see the light. __ I

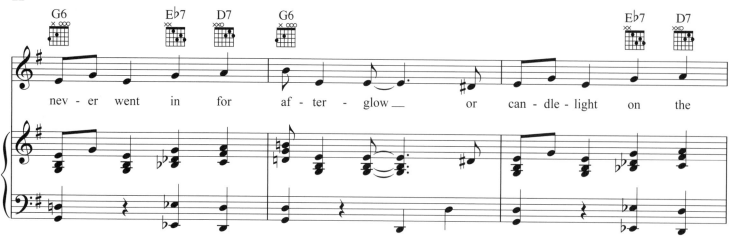

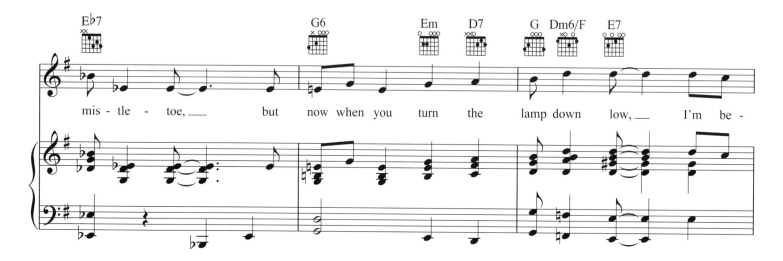

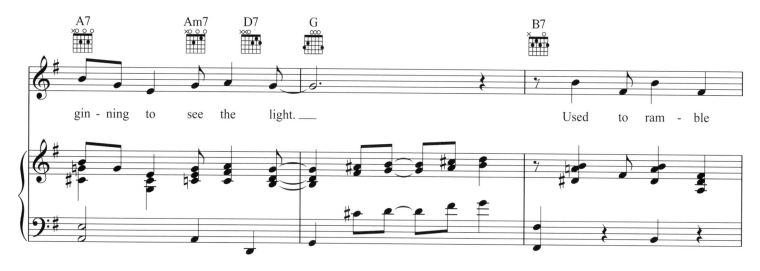

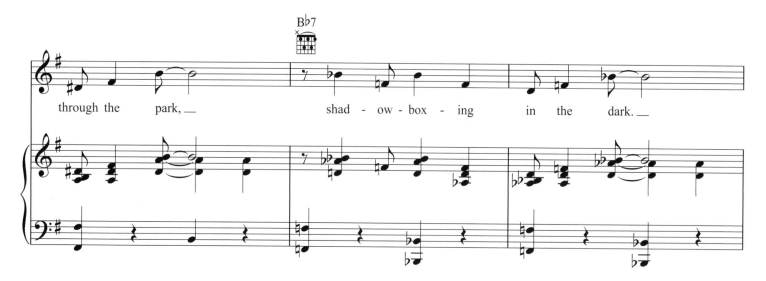

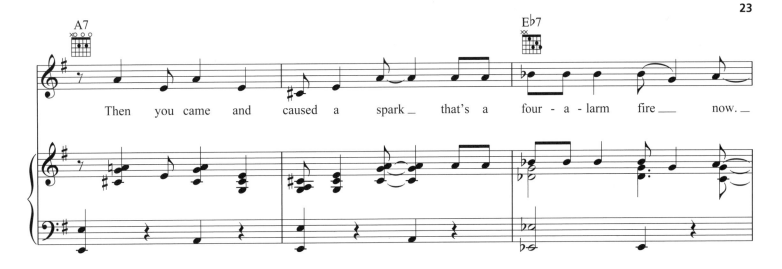

Then you came and caused a spark __ that's a four - a - larm fire __ now. __

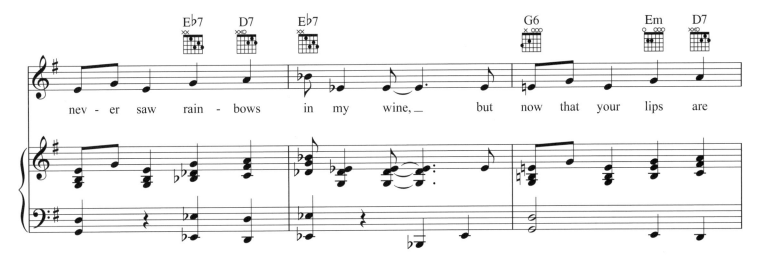

__ I nev - er made love by lan - tern shine, __ I

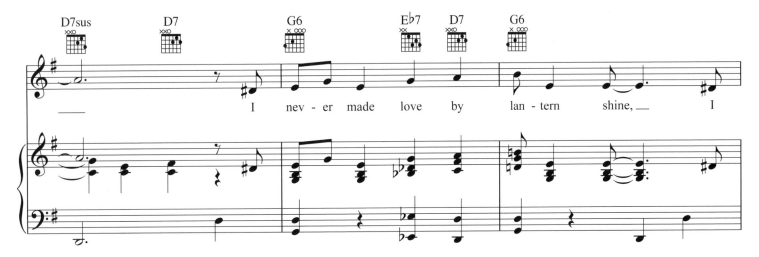

nev - er saw rain - bows in my wine, __ but now that your lips are

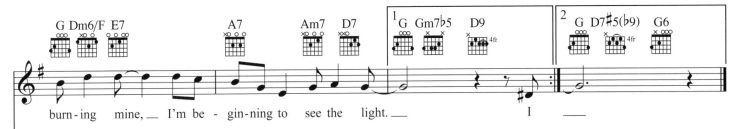

burn - ing mine, __ I'm be - gin - ning to see the light. __ I __

8vb

I LET A SONG GO OUT OF MY HEART

Words and Music by DUKE ELLINGTON,
HENRY NEMO, JOHN REDMOND
and IRVING MILLS

Slowly

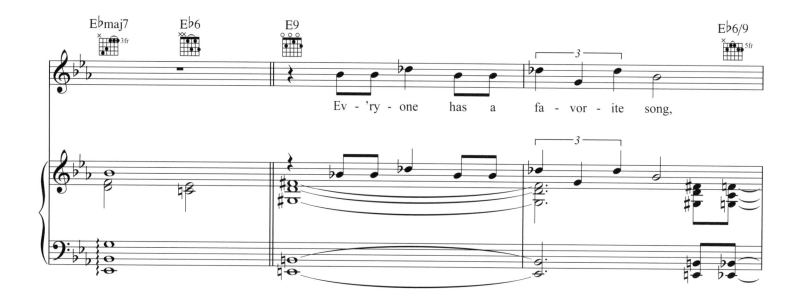

Ev - 'ry - one has a fa - vor - ite song,

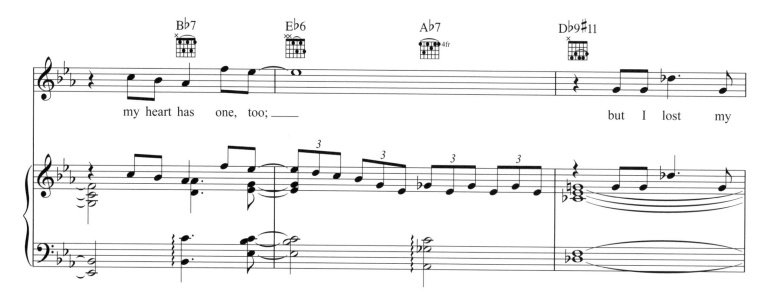

my heart has one, too; _____ but I lost my

drift-ed a-part life does-n't mean a thing to me.

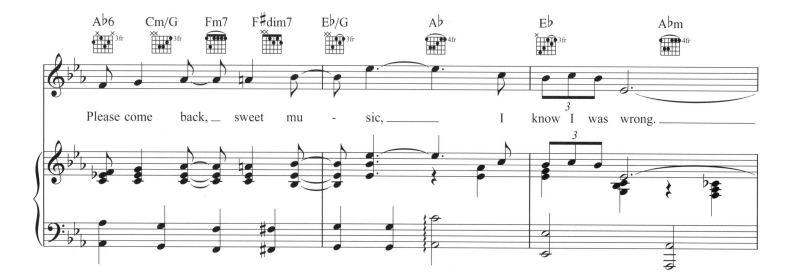

Please come back, sweet mu - sic, I know I was wrong.

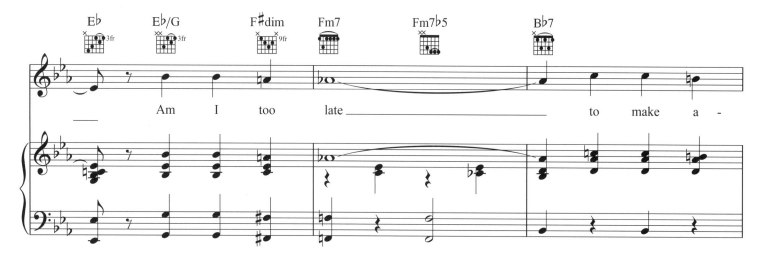

Am I too late to make a-

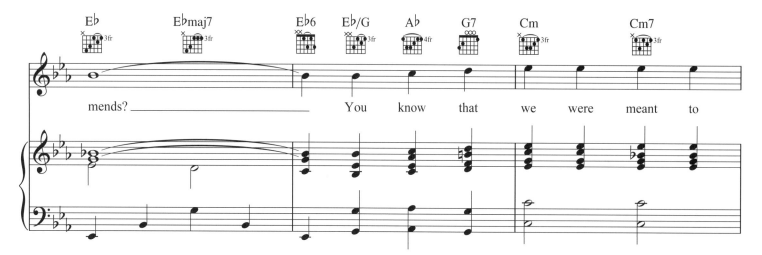

mends? You know that we were meant to

IN A MELLOW TONE

Words by MILT GABLER
Music by DUKE ELLINGTON

Medium Swing tempo

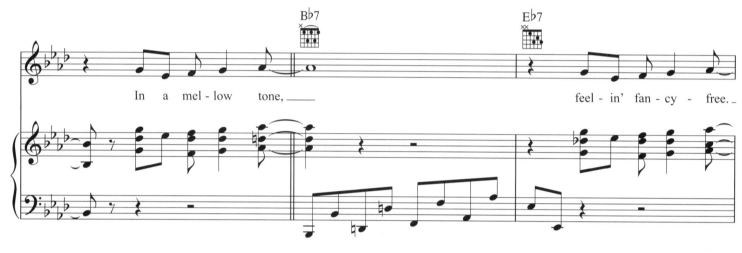

the live - long day. ___

With this mel - low song ___ I can't ___ go wrong. ___

In a mel - low tone, ___

that's the way to live. ___ If you mope and groan, ___

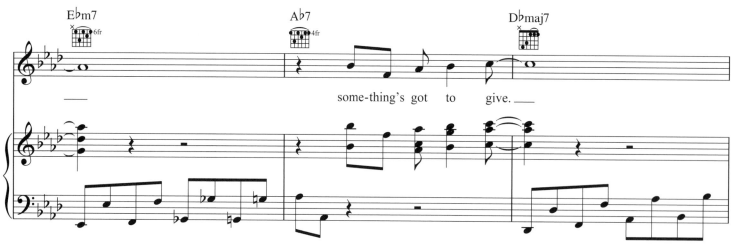

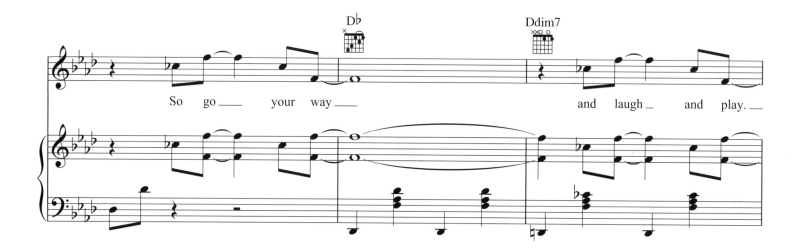

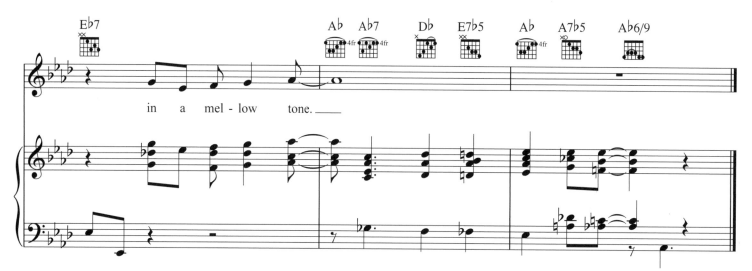

IN A SENTIMENTAL MOOD

Words and Music by DUKE ELLINGTON,
IRVING MILLS and MANNY KURTZ

Slowly, with expression

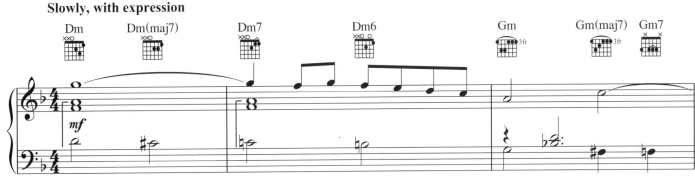

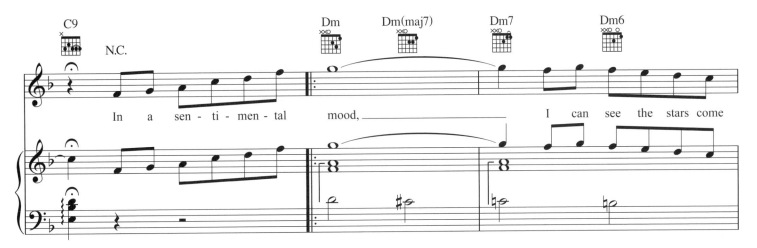

In a sen-ti-men-tal mood, _____ I can see the stars come

through my room, _____ while your lov-ing at-ti-tude _____ is like a

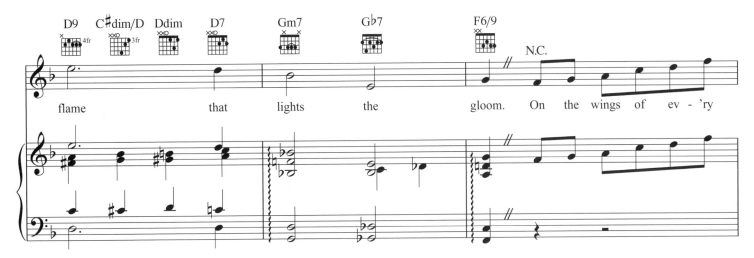

flame that lights the gloom. On the wings of ev-'ry

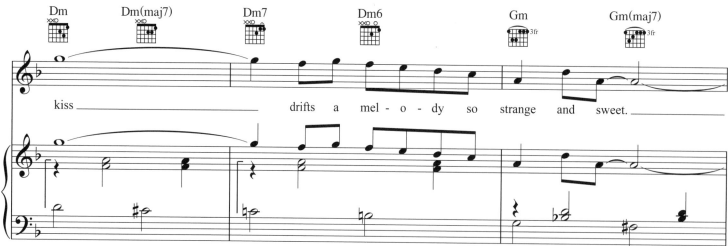

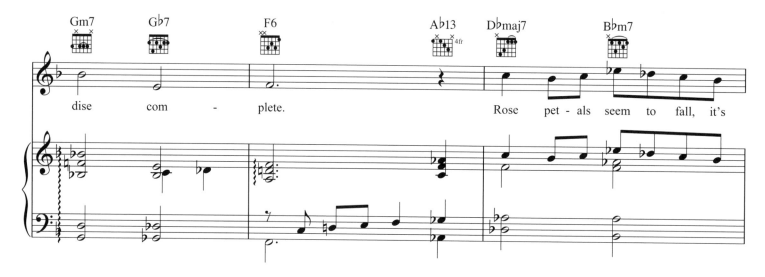

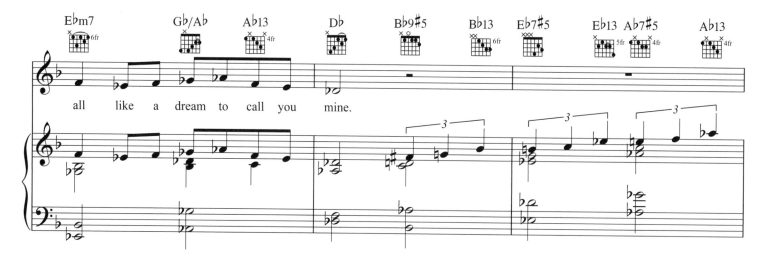

My heart's a light-er thing since you made this night a thing di-vine.

In a sen-ti-men-tal mood, _____ I'm with-in a world so

heav-en-ly, _____ for I nev-er dreamt that you'd _____ be lov-ing

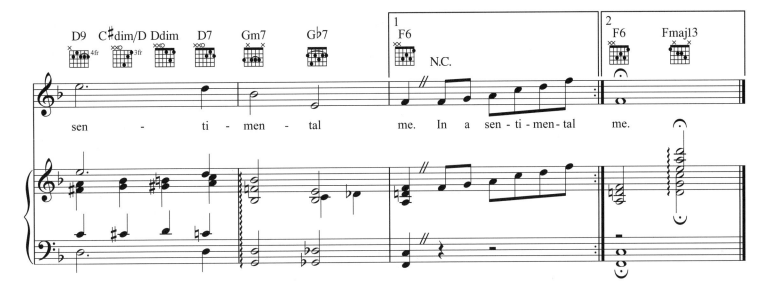

sen - ti - men - tal me. In a sen-ti-men-tal me.

IT DON'T MEAN A THING
(If It Ain't Got That Swing)

Words and Music by DUKE ELLINGTON
and IRVING MILLS

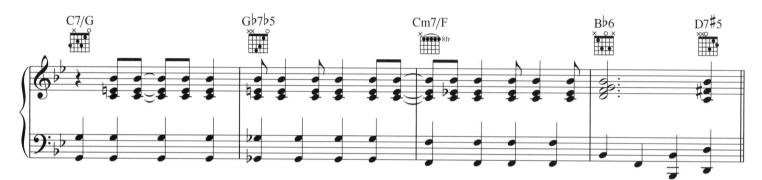

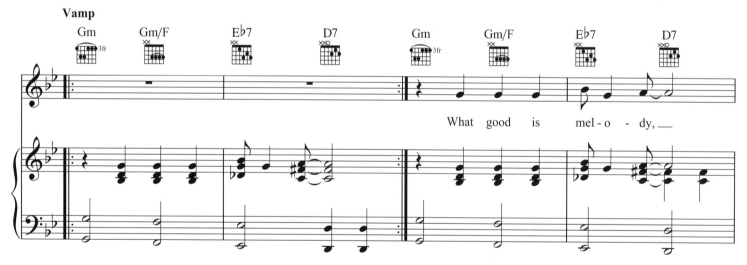

What good is mel-o-dy, ___

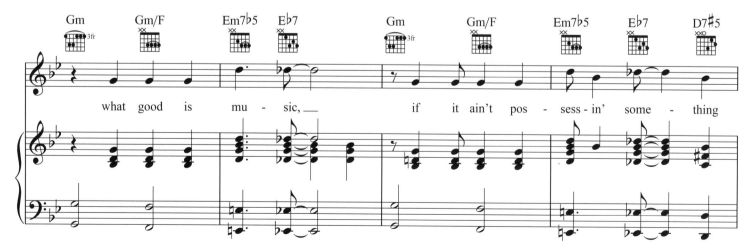

what good is mu-sic, ___ if it ain't pos-sess-in' some-thing

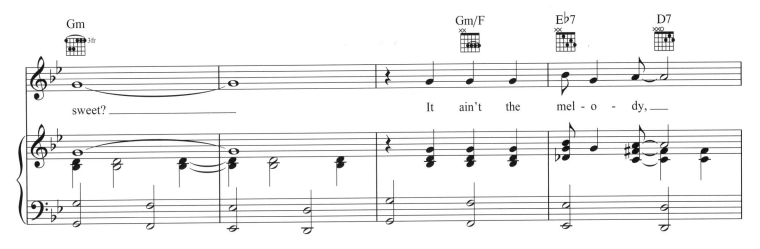

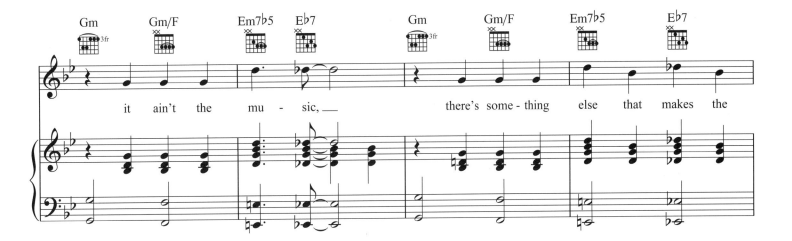

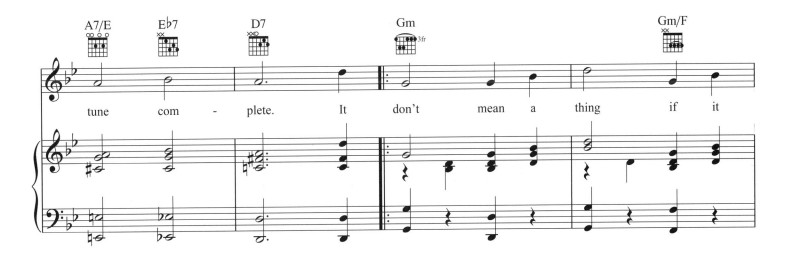

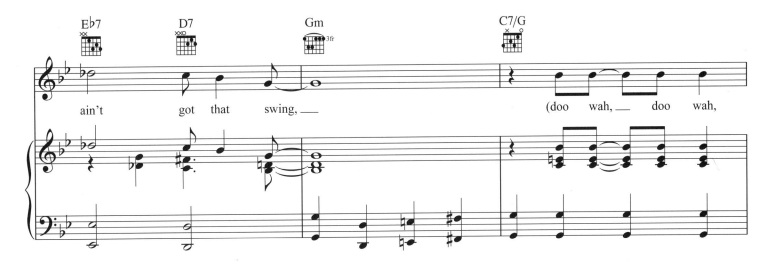

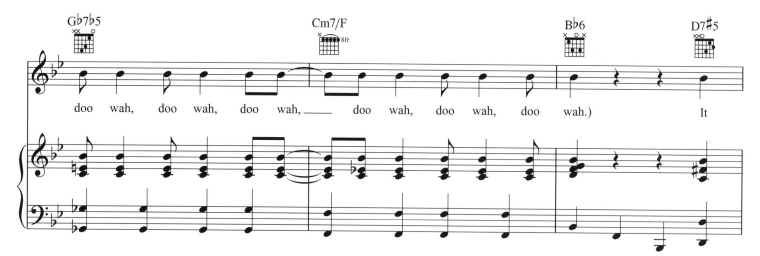

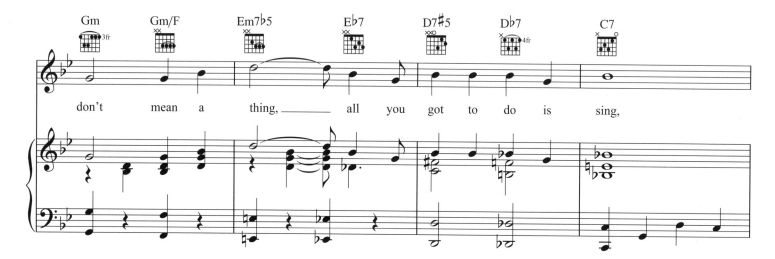

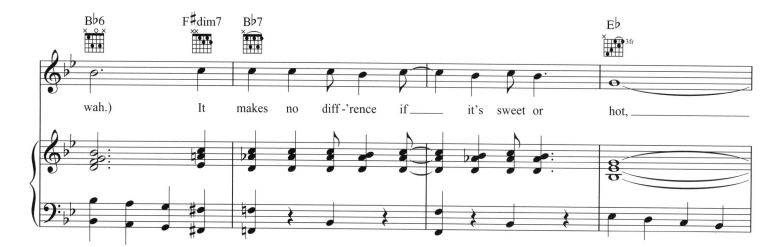

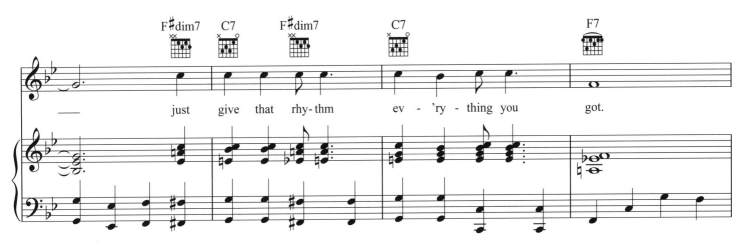

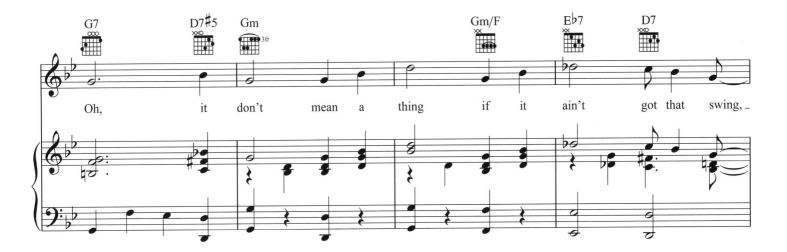

LOVE YOU MADLY

By DUKE ELLINGTON

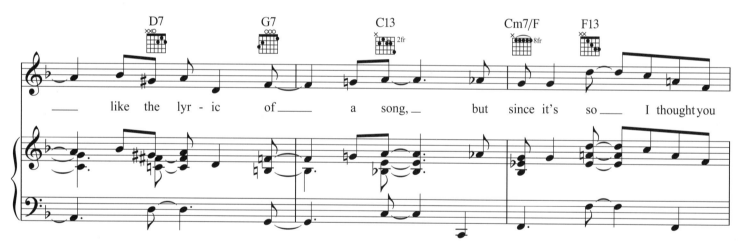

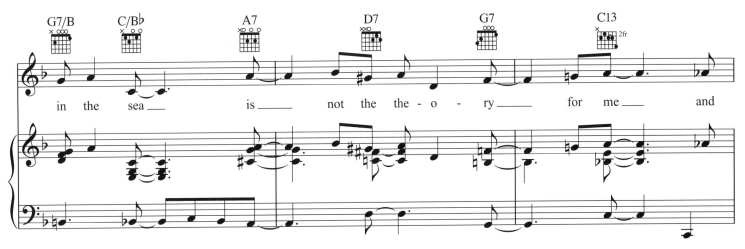

in the sea ___ is ___ not the the-o-ry ___ for me ___ and

that's for sure. ___ Just like I said be-fore, ___ "I love you, love ___ you mad-

- ly." If you could see the hap-py you and me ___ I

dream a-bout so proud - ly, ___ you'd know the breath of spring ___ that

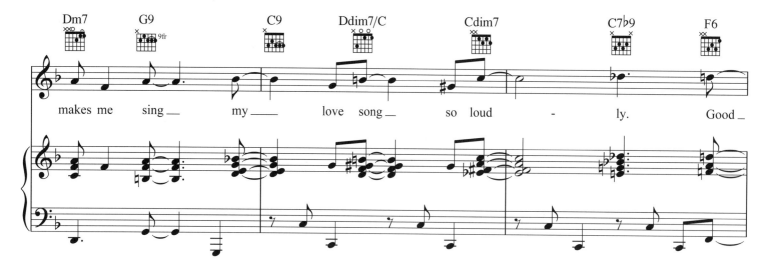

makes me sing __ my __ love song __ so loud - ly. Good __

__ things come to those who wait, __ so __ just re - lax and wait __

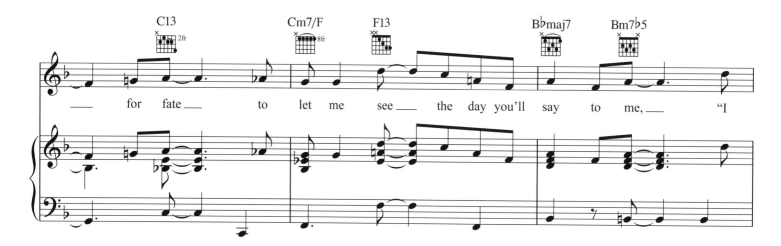

__ for fate __ to let me see __ the day you'll say to me, __ "I

love you, love __ you mad - ly!" Love__ - ly!"

SATIN DOLL

Words by JOHNNY MERCER,
BILLY STRAYHORN and DUKE ELLINGTON
Music by DUKE ELLINGTON

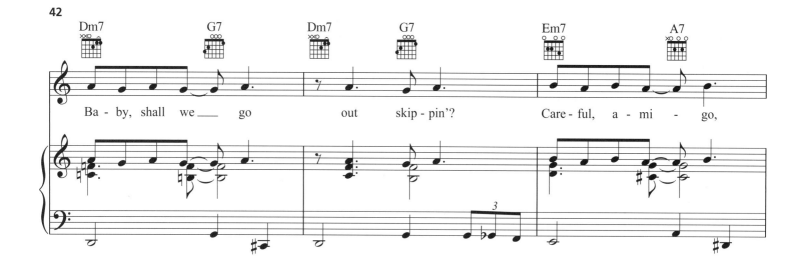

Ba - by, shall we __ go out skip - pin'? Care - ful, a - mi - go,

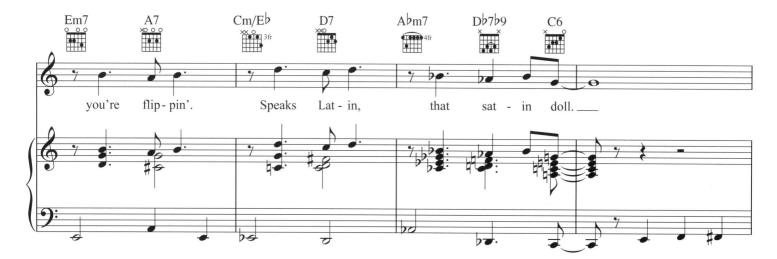

you're flip - pin'. Speaks Lat - in, that sat - in doll. __

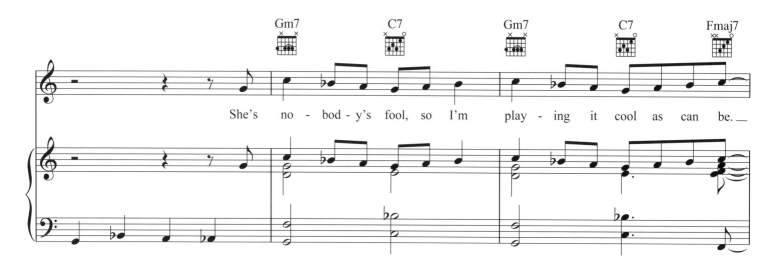

She's no - bod - y's fool, so I'm play - ing it cool as can be. __

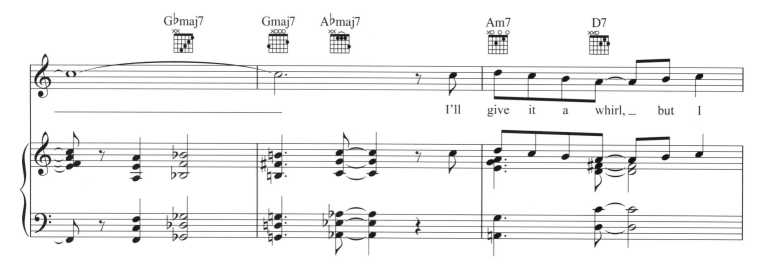

I'll give it a whirl, __ but I

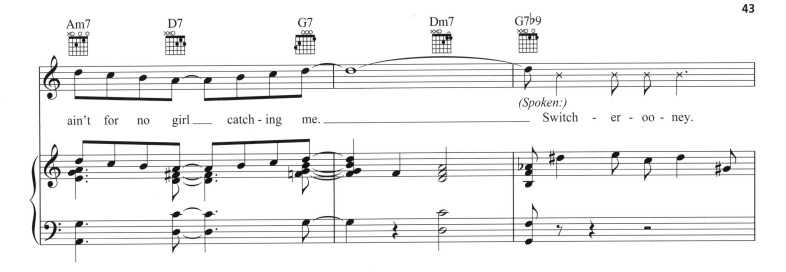

ain't for no girl ___ catch - ing me. _____ *(Spoken:)* Switch - er - oo - ney.

Tel - e - phone num - bers well you know, do - ing my rhum - bas

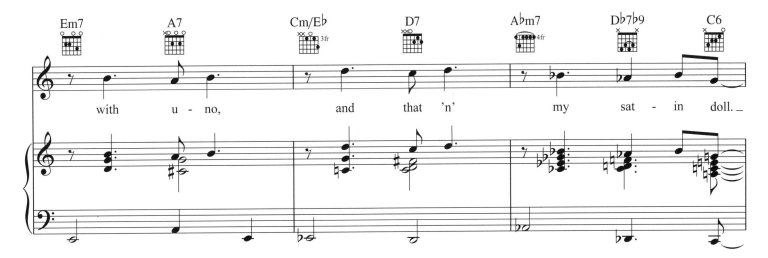

with u - no, and that 'n' my sat - in doll. _

MOOD INDIGO

Words and Music by DUKE ELLINGTON,
IRVING MILLS and ALBANY BIGARD

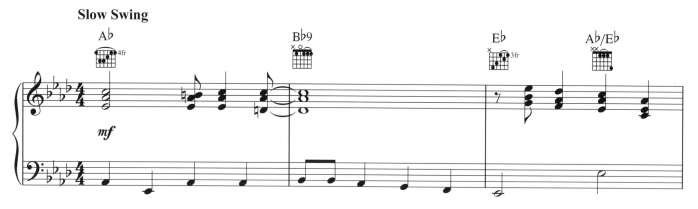

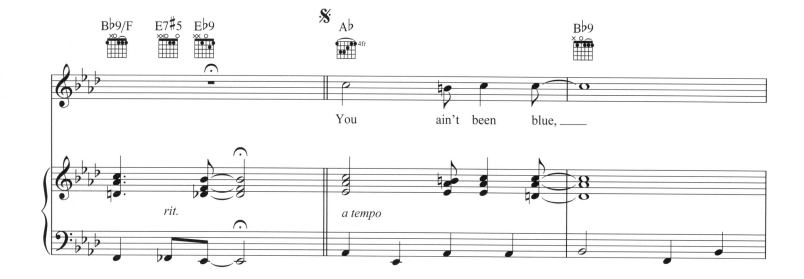

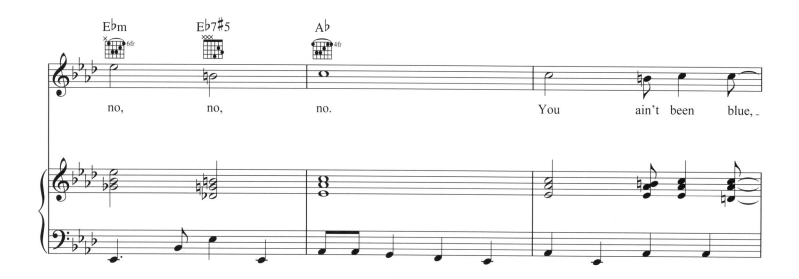

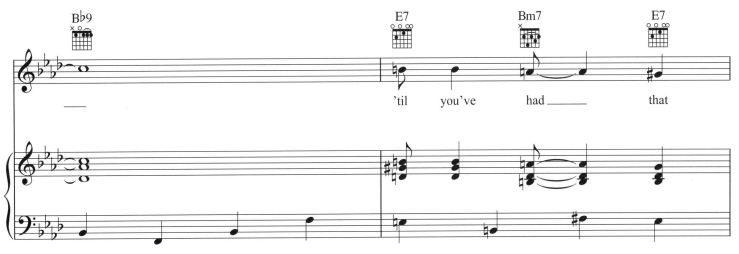

'til you've had _____ that

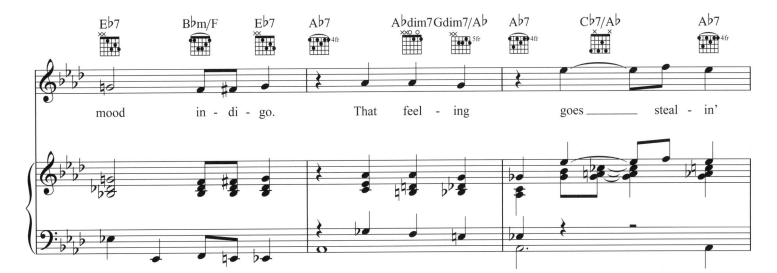

mood in - di - go. That feel - ing goes _____ steal - in'

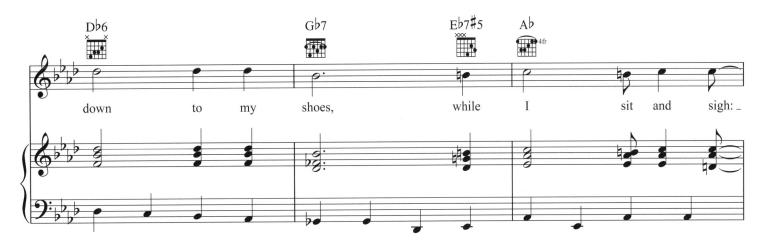

down to my shoes, while I sit and sigh: __

To Coda ⊕

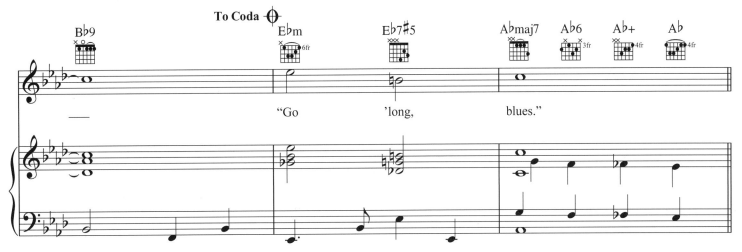

"Go 'long, blues."

46

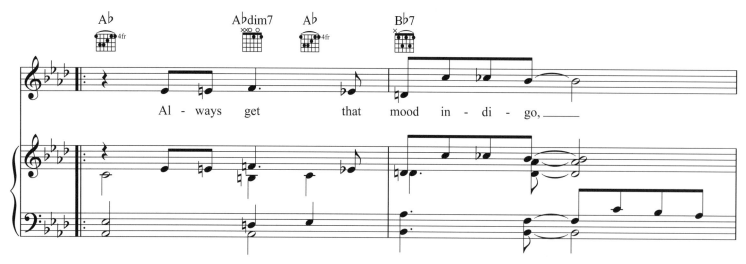

Al - ways get that mood in - di - go,____

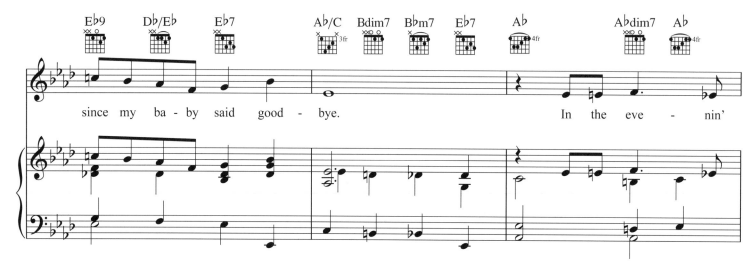

since my ba - by said good - bye.   In the eve - nin'

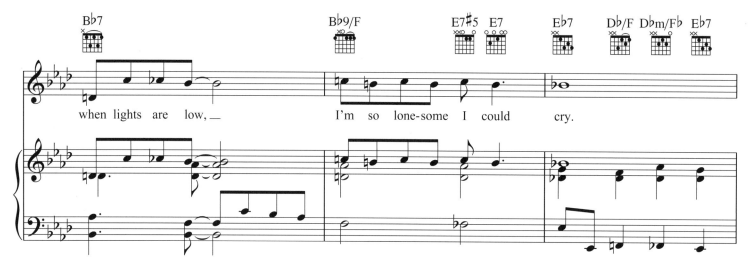

when lights are low,__   I'm so lone-some I could   cry.

'Cause there's no - bod - y   who   cares a - bout me,____

I'm just a soul who's blu - er than blue ___ can be.

When I get that mood in - di - go, ___

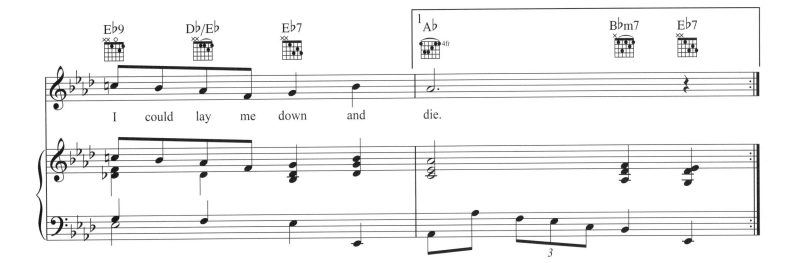

I could lay me down and die.

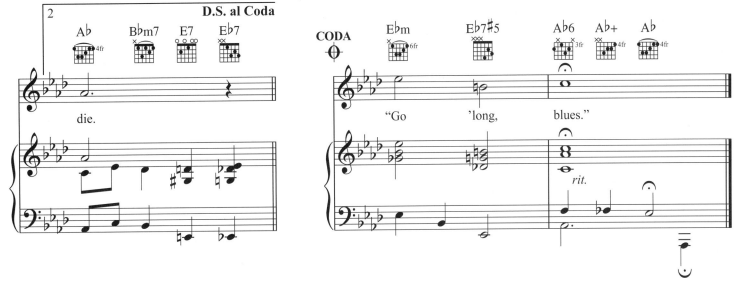

die.

CODA

"Go 'long, blues."

SOLITUDE

Words and Music by DUKE ELLINGTON,
EDDIE DE LANGE and IRVING MILLS

Slowly, with expression

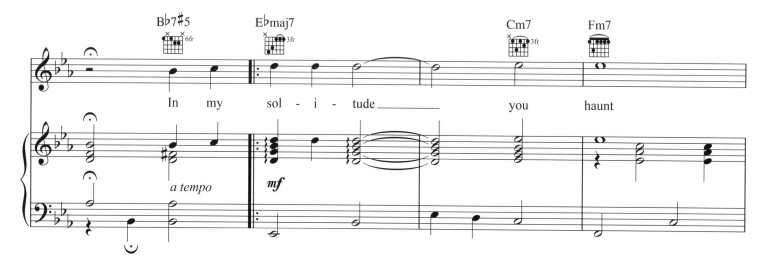

In my sol - i - tude _____ you haunt

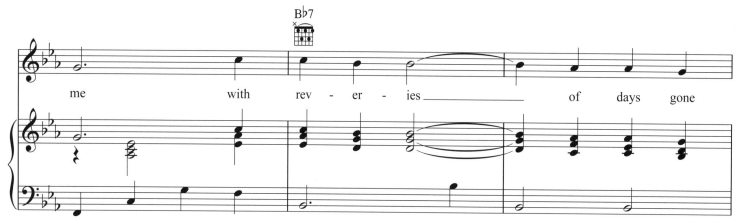

me with rev - er - ies _____ of days gone

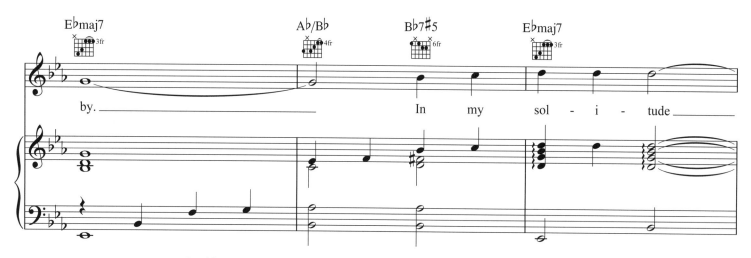

by. _____ In my sol - i - tude _____

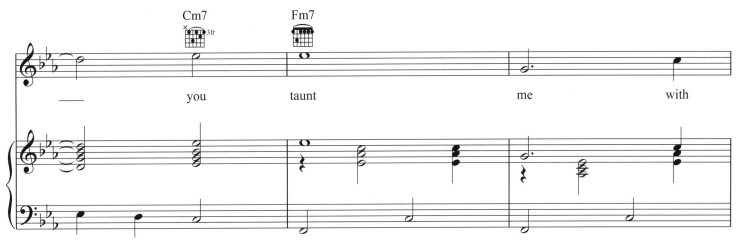

you taunt me with

mem - o - ries _____ that nev - er die. _____

_____ I sit in my chair, I'm filled with de - spair, there's

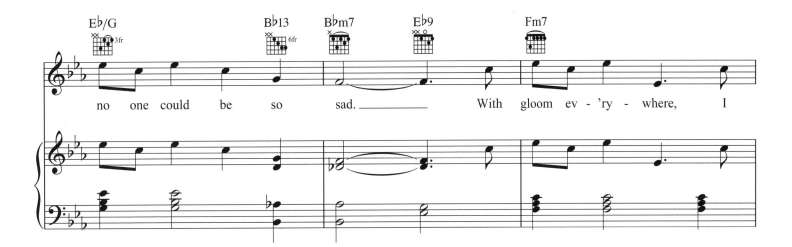

no one could be so sad. _____ With gloom ev - 'ry - where, I

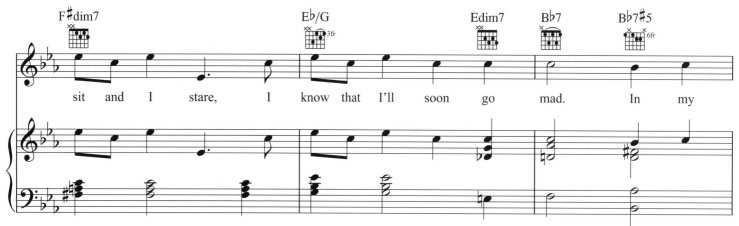

sit and I stare, I know that I'll soon go mad. In my

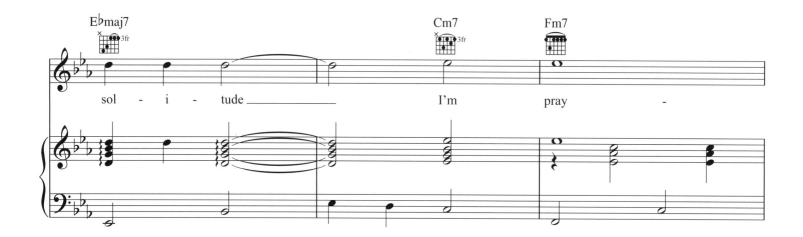

sol - i - tude _____ I'm pray -

ing, dear Lord a - bove, _____ send back my

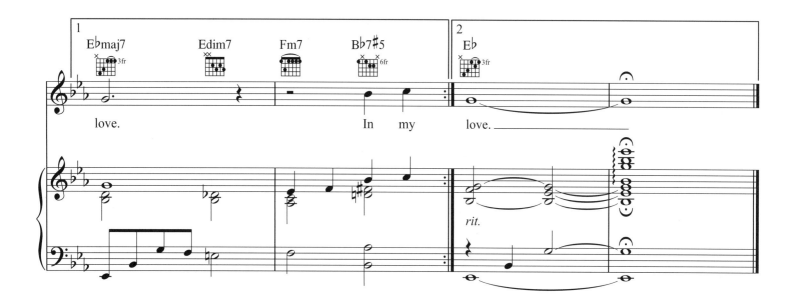

love. In my love. _____

SOPHISTICATED LADY

Words and Music by DUKE ELLINGTON,
IRVING MILLS and MITCHELL PARISH

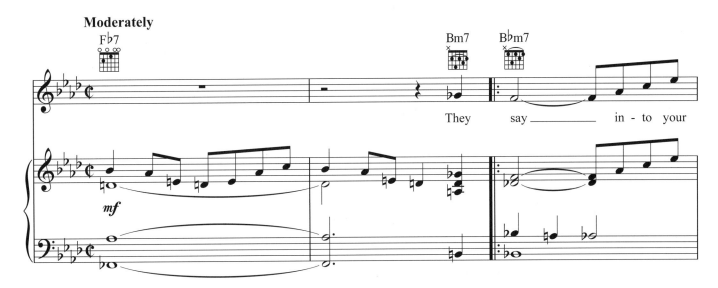

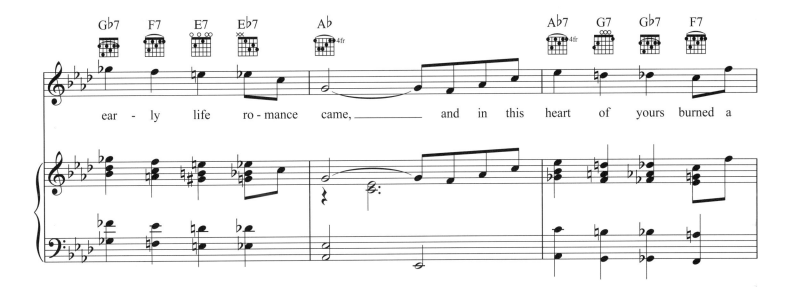

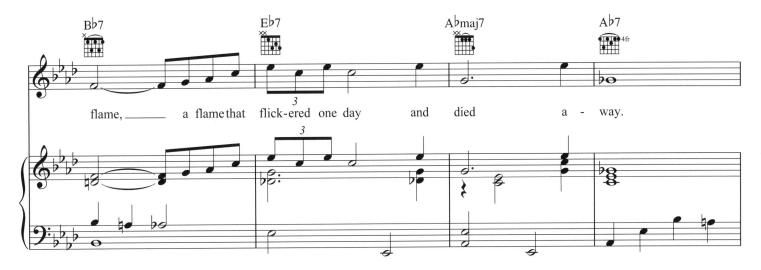

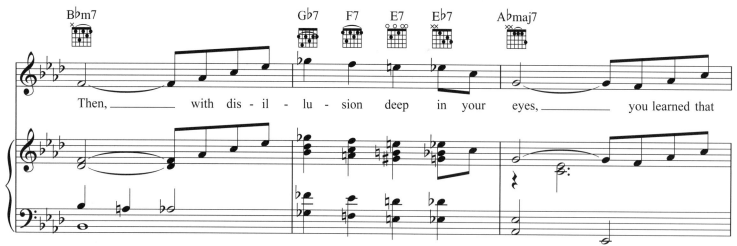

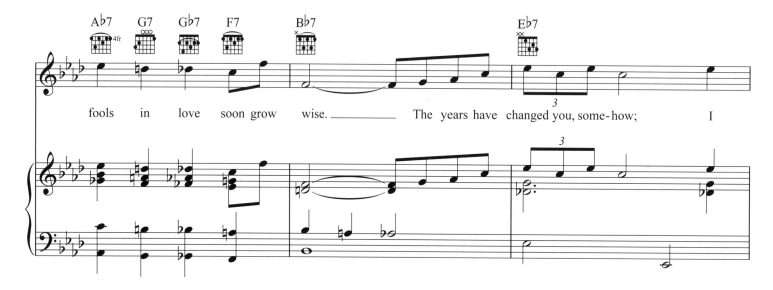

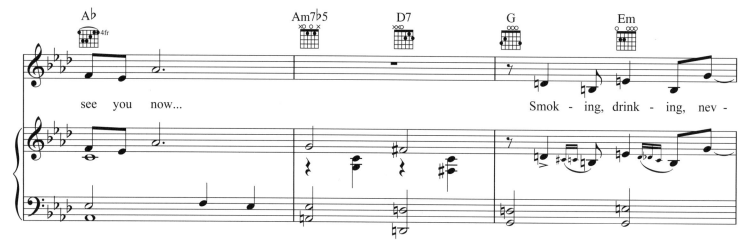

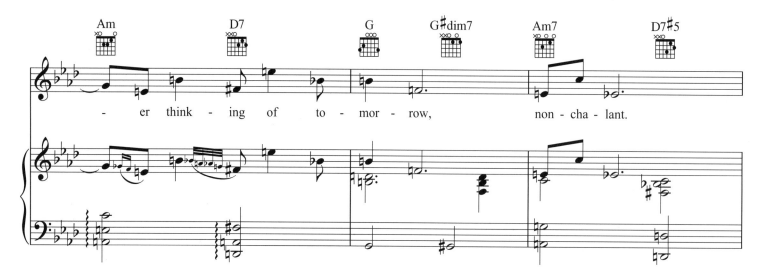

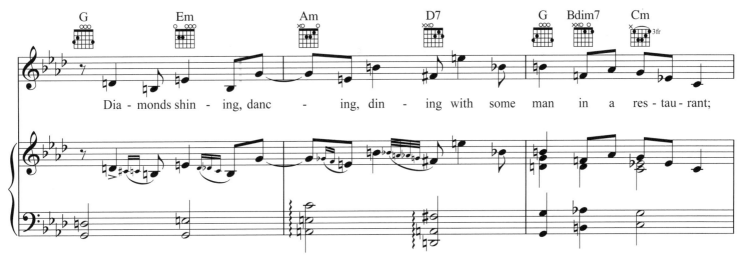

Dia - monds shin - ing, danc - - ing, din - ing with some man in a res - tau - rant;

is that all you real - ly want? No, ____ So - phis - ti - cat - ed la - dy, I

know, ____ you miss the love you lost long a - go, ____ and when no - bod - y is nigh you

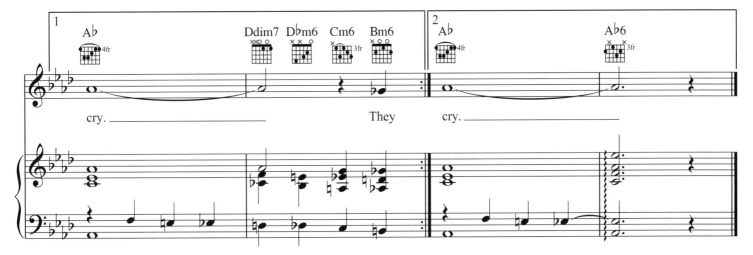

cry. ____ They cry. ____

TAKE THE "A" TRAIN

Words and Music by
BILLY STRAYHORN

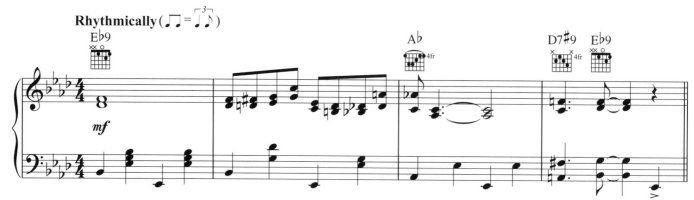

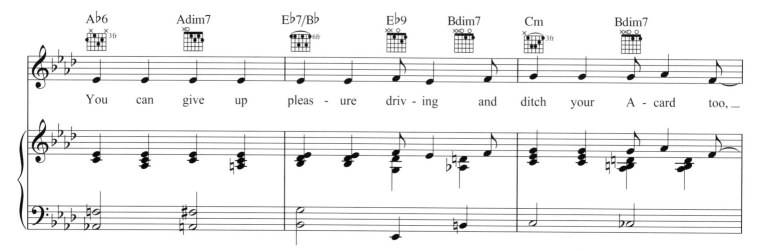

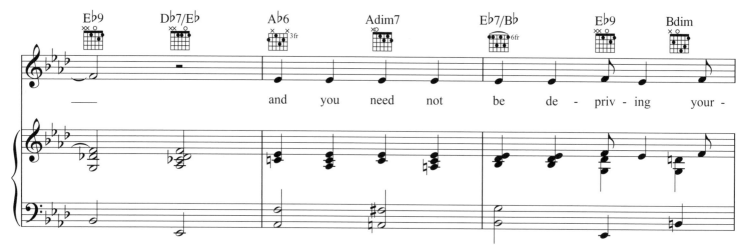

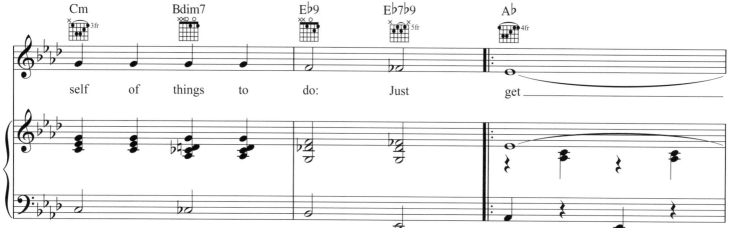

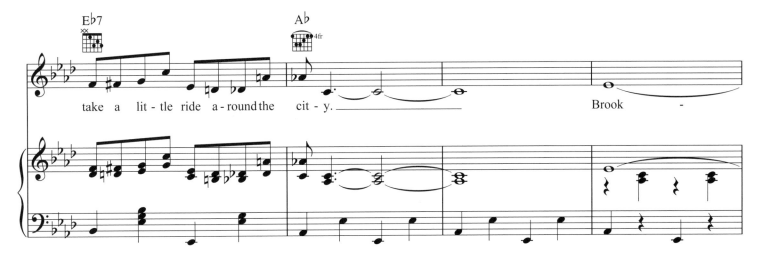

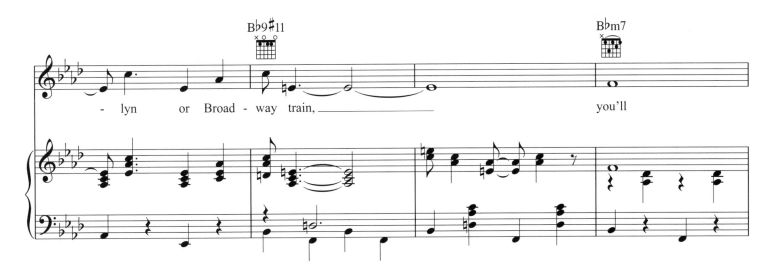

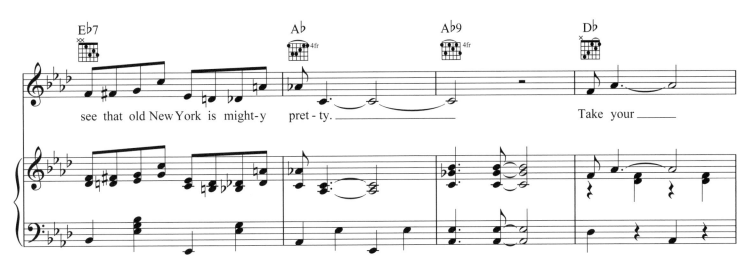

ba-by sub-way rid-ing. _____ That's where _____ ro-mance may be

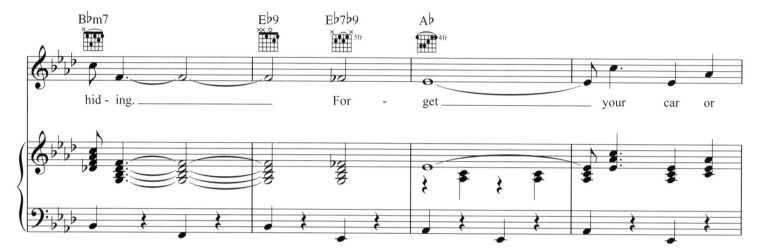

hid - ing. _____ For - get _____ your car or

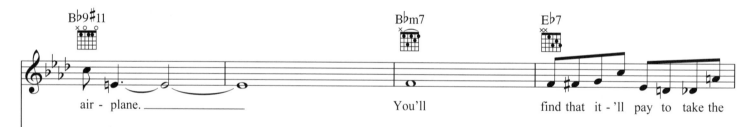

air - plane. _____ You'll find that it -'ll pay to take the

"A" train. _____ "A" train. _____